A Little Book of ...

Also available in the same series:

A Little Book of Daily Prayer

Compiled by Tony Castle

Marshall Pickering

An Imprint of HarperCollins*Publishers*

Dedicated to Elizabeth
Proverbs 31:10

Marshall Pickering is an Imprint of
HarperCollins*Religious*
Part of HarperCollins*Publishers*
77–85 Fulham Palace Road, London W6 8JB

First published in Great Britain
in 1996 by Marshall Pickering

1 3 5 7 9 10 8 6 4 2

Copyright © 1996 Tony Castle

Tony Castle asserts the moral right to be
identified as the compiler of this work

A catalogue record for this book is
available from the British Library

ISBN 0 551 02995 1

Printed and bound in Great Britain by
Woolnough Bookbinding Ltd, Irthlingborough, Northamptonshire

CONDITIONS OF SALE

Contents

Introduction

Prayer is the very life-blood of the Christian. No one can claim to be a Christian without having an active and personal relationship with God, in and through Christ.

As a young child I was taught that prayer is 'the raising of the mind and heart to God'. Time has passed and I have learned to appreciate and try to live by that simple and accurate description. Being able to raise our minds and hearts to God marks us out as distinctively human. Prayer is therefore more about the direction and orientation of human life, with all its joys and sorrows, than aiming wordy formulas heavenward.

How often should we pray? The established Jewish practice, at the time of Christ, was to pray at the third, sixth and ninth hours (the sixth hour being midday). The devout Muslim prays five times a day.

It was certainly the teaching of Jesus that his followers should pray regularly and often (Luke 18:1). This teaching was developed by Paul, who urged his readers to 'pray in the Spirit on all occasions' (Ephesians 6:18) and to 'pray continually' (1 Thessalonians 5:17).

Clearly prayer has never been understood as an adjunct to life, something tacked on to a busy day, if and when there's time. It is at the very centre of life, the core from which all else springs and is nourished. This was appreciated from the very beginning of Christianity. According to John Henry Newman, 'The Jewish observance of the third, sixth and ninth hours of prayer, was continued by the inspired founders of the Christian Church.' By the end of the fifth century a structure of daily prayer at seven times of the day had been developed by the Monastic Orders which were gaining in strength and popularity; starting with Matins and Lauds in the morning and ending the day with Vespers and Compline. Prime, Terce, and Sext were spread throughout the day.

This little book offers a very simple form of daily prayer drawn from the most ancient practices of the Church as recorded in the Bible and in history. It is almost entirely based on Scripture, and therefore accessible to Christians of all traditions.

'Where your treasure is, there your heart will be also' (Matthew 6:21). If Christ is our treasure then our hearts will be in prayer, prayer which gives our lives meaning and purpose.

Tony Castle
Harvest 1995

Using This Book

The purpose of this book is to make itself redundant. It is intended to be a simple introduction to praying throughout the day in the ancient and traditional style of following the 'Hours' of the Prayer of the Church. It is my hope that, after a time, once you have become accustomed to the format and the self-discipline involved, you will want to move on to use a fuller version.

Start by using 'Morning Prayer' (some people only use Morning and Night Prayer) just as it is laid out. After a while you will feel the need to freshen your Morning Prayer by changing the psalm, the poem or the reading. There are a number of alternatives provided or you can open your Bible and select other readings or

psalms. Likewise in Advent or Lent, change
the poem, the reading and the prayer to fit the
season.

To supplement your Morning Prayer, or to
make a change from it, you could use material from
the selection of individual prayers.

Making time for prayer is often a problem. The
solution is to always remember that prayer-time is
meeting-with-a-friend-time. If we can spend twenty
minutes chatting on the phone to a friend, then we
can easily put aside five minutes to speak to the
most important friend of all.

Adapting your routine is another answer. If
there is insufficient time in your present morning
programme, get up five or ten minutes earlier
– just as you might if you were going out for the
day with a friend. Where there's a will, there's a
way, and once you begin to discover the difference
that regular prayer makes, you will find yourself
naturally longing for more.

Morning Prayer:
A Simple Pattern

Written prayer, even from the Bible, exists for only one purpose, to stimulate and lead us into our own awareness of God and communication with him. We must never feel obliged to read, use or follow any written format or pattern of prayer. A single line or phrase may prompt a personal response to God — go with it, abandon the rest of the written text.

A sense of duty too can reap a rich reward. Praying faithfully each morning, even when the written words cease to spark a response, when the mind wanders and it all feels dull and routine, is to acknowledge that prayer is two-way. The faithfulness, the loyalty and commitment is appreciated, without any doubt, by the recipient. Our Father hears all prayer and prayer never goes unanswered.

In the following simple order of Morning Prayer, the brief opening sentence from the Psalms (prayers used by Jesus himself) is intended to stimulate an awareness of God's presence. The act of adoration of the Holy Trinity acknowledges our dependence upon Father, Son and Holy Spirit. The poem is offered as a pause for reflection and perhaps a stimulus to personal prayer. With the psalm we join in the prayer of the whole Christian Church, for the Psalms are used daily all around the world by Christians of every tradition to praise God.

The Bible reading is intended to direct our attention to a particular season or theme, while the traditional use of the canticle of Zechariah continues an ancient and widespread Christian practice. The prayers of intercession are necessarily general ones and can be, or even should be, replaced by personal petitions and concerns.

Morning Prayer

You have made known to me the path of life;
you will fill me with joy in your presence.

Psalm 16:11

Adoration

O God the Father,
  who has wonderfully created out of nothing,
  who governs and maintains the universe with
    your power,
  who surrendered your Son to death for us,
  – your majesty is unspeakable,
  – your power is incomparable,
  – your goodness is immeasurable.

O God the Son,
  who was born of the virgin,
  who has washed us in your precious blood,

who conquered death by your victorious rising,
— your majesty is unspeakable,
— your power is incomparable,
— your goodness is immeasurable.

O God the Holy Spirit,
who descended upon Jesus as a dove,
who appeared above the Apostles as tongues
of fire,
who visits and strengthens the hearts of
believers.
— your majesty is unspeakable,
— your power is incomparable,
— your goodness is immeasurable.

O Blessed Trinity,   Father so good,
Son so loving,
Spirit so kind,
your work is life
your love is grace

your contemplation is glory.
You I worship.
You I acknowledge with all the love of my heart.

Lancelot Andrewes

Poem

It is done.
Once again the Fire has penetrated the earth.
Not with the sudden crash of thunderbolt,
riving the mountain tops:
does the Master break down doors to enter his own
  home?
Without earthquake, or thunderclap:
the flame has lit up the whole world from within.
All things individually and collectively
are penetrated and flooded by it,
from the inmost core of the tiniest atom
to the mighty sweep of the most universal laws of
  being:

so naturally has it flooded every element, every
  energy,
every connecting link in the unity of our cosmos,
that one might suppose the cosmos to have burst
spontaneously into flame.

Pierre Teilhard de Chardin

The Psalm

Psalm 145:1–5,8–9

The Lord is gracious and compassionate,
slow to anger and rich in love.

I will exalt you, my God the King;
I will praise your name for ever and ever.
Every day I will praise you
and extol your name for ever and ever.

Great is the Lord and most worthy of praise;
his greatness no one can fathom.

One generation will commend your works to
    another;
they will tell of your mighty acts.
They will speak of the glorious
splendour of your majesty,
and I will meditate on your wonderful works.

The Lord is gracious and compassionate,
slow to anger and rich in love.
The Lord is good to all;
he has compassion on all he has made.

**The Lord is gracious and compassionate,
slow to anger and rich in love.**

See page 70 for alternative psalms

The Word of God

I kneel before the Father, from whom his whole
family in heaven and earth derives its name. I pray
that out of his glorious riches he may strengthen
you with power through his Spirit in your inner
being, so that Christ may dwell in your hearts
through faith. And I pray that you, being rooted and
established in love, may have power, together with
all the saints, to grasp how wide and long and high
and deep is the love of Christ, and to know this love
that surpasses knowledge – that you may be filled to
the measure of all the fullness of God.

Ephesians 3:14–19

See page 80 for alternative readings

The Canticle of Zechariah

Luke 1:68–75

Great is the Lord and most worthy of praise;
his greatness no one can fathom.

Praise be to the Lord, the God of Israel,
because he has come and has redeemed his people.

He has raised up a horn of salvation for us
in the house of his servant David
(as he said through his prophets of long ago),

Salvation from our enemies
and from the hand of all who hate us –
to show mercy to our fathers
and to remember his holy covenant.

The oath he swore to our father Abraham:
to rescue us from the hand of our enemies,

and to enable us to serve him without fear
in holiness and righteousness before him all our days.

Great is the Lord and most worthy of praise,
his greatness no one can fathom.

Prayers of Intercession

To be used as a basis for your own intercession.

Almighty God, the heavens cannot contain your
greatness; yet your Son has taught us to call you,
Abba Father. We have learned to say:
Father, may your kingdom come.

We praise and love you as your children; may we
respect and honour your name today. May all
people learn to say:
Father, may your kingdom come.

Give us today the courage to forgive others — as you constantly forgive us. So that with clear hearts we can say:
Father, may your kingdom come.

Be with us, Father, as we face the anxieties and temptations of this day; do not allow us to fall away from you. May we always sincerely pray:
Father, may your kingdom come.

Closing Prayer

Almighty Father,
shed the light of your love
over the day that lies ahead;
may every thought, word and action
become a worthy offering to you,
to give you glory
and further your kingdom. Amen.

A Selection of Morning Prayers

Ever since the women friends of Jesus, 'very early in the morning' on the third day, found the tomb empty, the early morning has been a special time of prayer for Christians. After the dark stillness of night, the rising of the sun is so reminiscent of the rising of the Son that it has always seemed natural for Christ's followers to offer each new day, in union with him, to the Father. Each new day brings new life and new opportunities to unite with the Risen Lord in his eternal offering of praise.

The Lord's Prayer

Our Father in heaven,
hallowed be your name,
your kingdom come,
your will be done,
on earth as in heaven.
Give us today our daily bread.
Forgive us our sins
as we forgive those who sin against us.
Lead us not into temptation
but deliver us from evil.

For the kingdom, the power
and the glory are yours,
now and for ever. Amen.

This prayer, given to us by Jesus himself, should form part of any compilation of prayers used each morning. Throughout the ages all devout Christians have found this prayer a daily inspiration.

What deep mysteries, my dearest brothers, are contained in the Lord's Prayer.

Saint Cyprian

The Lord's Prayer is the prayer above all prayers.

Martin Luther

The sublime perfection of this evangelical prayer is marvellous and we ought to thank God fervently for it.

Saint Teresa of Avila

It is said that in the meditative use of the Lord's Prayer, Saint Teresa of Avila could never get beyond the first line.

Other Morning Prayers

O God our Father, thank you for waking me to see
the light of this new day. Grant that I may waste
none of its hours; soil none of its moments; neglect
none of its opportunities; fail in none of its duties.
And bring me to the evening time undefeated by
any temptation, at peace with myself, and with you.
This I ask for your love's sake.

William Barclay

O Lord my God,
teach my heart this day where and how to see you,
where and how to find you.
Teach me to see you,
for I cannot seek you
unless you teach me,
or find you
unless you show yourself to me.

Saint Anselm of Canterbury

O Lord, when I awake and day begins
waken me to your presence;
waken me to your indwelling;
waken me to inward sight of you,
and speech with you
and strength from you;
that all my earthly walk may waken into song
and my spirit leap up to you all day,
all ways.

Eric Milner-White

We give you heartfelt thanks, heavenly Father, for
the rest of the past night, and for the gift of a new
day with its opportunities of living to your glory.
May we so pass its hours in the perfect freedom of
your service that, when evening comes, we may
again give you thanks; through Jesus Christ our
Lord.

Orthodox Liturgy

Lord Jesus, I thank you; you have watched over and protected me, your unworthy servant, with your loving presence all through the night. You have brought me safe and unharmed to this morning hour. I thank you for all the blessings you have given, of your great goodness, to me.

Saint Edmund of Abingdon

Eternal God, who knows neither morning nor evening, yet wraps us in love both night and day, lift the curtain of night from the world and the veil from our hearts. Rise with your morning sun upon our souls and enliven our work and prayer. May we walk this day in the steps of him who worked in harmony with your will. Amen.

James Martineau

I want to begin this day with thankfulness, and
    continue it with eagerness.
I shall be busy; let me set about things in the spirit of

17

service to you and to my fellows, that Jesus knew
in the carpenter's shop in Nazareth.
I am glad that he drew no line between work sacred
and secular.

Take the skill that resides in my hands, and use it
today;
Take the experience that life has given me, and
use it;
Keep my eyes open, and my imagination alert, that I
may see how things look to others, especially the
unwell, the worried, the overworked. For your
love's sake. Amen.

Rita Snowden

Living each day to the full,
Lord, let me live this day
as if it were my first day,
or my last.
Let me bring to it

all the wonder and amazement of a new-born child;
the trust
that welcomes all I meet,
expects of them only the best,
and grant them the benefit
of every possible doubt;
But let me also bring
the wisdom and experience of the aged to this day;
the tenderness
that grows from years of care and gently giving;
the hope
that has been forged through all the fires of doubt.

J. Barrie Shepherd

O God, I know that I am going to be very busy
today. Help me not to be so busy that I miss the
most important things.

Help me not to be too busy to look up and to see a
glimpse of beauty in your world.

Help me not to be too busy listening to other voices
to hear your voice when you speak to me.

Help me not to be too busy to listen to anyone who
is in trouble, and to help anyone who is in
difficulty.

Help me not to be too busy to stand still for a
moment to think and to remember.

Help me not to be too busy to remember the claims
of my home, my children and my family.

Help me all through today to remember that I must
work my hardest, and also to remember that
sometimes I must be still.

This I ask for Jesus' sake. Amen.

William Barclay

Midday Prayer:
A Simple Pattern

The Apostle Paul encourages his friends at Ephesus to 'pray in the spirit on all occasions' (Ephesians 5:17), and those at Thessalonica he urged to 'pray continually' (1 Thessalonians 5:17). To remember to stop in the middle of a busy day and set aside a few precious minutes is not only to heed Paul's sound advice but to demonstrate real love of God. We can give God nothing more precious than our time.

Midday Prayer

Lord, open my lips to proclaim your praise.
To you be glory in the Church and in the world
from generation to generation evermore. Amen.

Invocation to the Holy Spirit

O Come, O Holy Spirit, come.
Come as holy fire and warm us,
Come as holy wind and cleanse us,
Come as holy light and lead us,
Come as holy truth and teach us,
Come as holy forgiveness and free us,
Come as holy love and enfold us,
Come as holy power and enable us,
Come as holy life and dwell in us.
Convict us, convert us, consecrate us,
until we are wholly Thine for Thy using,
through Jesus Christ our Lord.

Ancient Prayer

The Psalm

Psalm 121

The Lord will keep you from all harm.

I lift up my eyes to the hills —
where does my help come from?
My help comes from the Lord,
the Maker of heaven and earth.

He will not let your foot slip —
he who watches over you will not slumber;
indeed, he who watches over Israel
will neither slumber nor sleep.

The Lord watches over you —
the Lord is your shade at your right hand;
the sun will not harm you by day,
nor the moon by night.

The Lord will keep you from all harm —
he will watch over your life;
the Lord will watch over your coming and going
both now and for evermore.

The Lord will keep you from all harm.

The Word of God

You were once darkness, but now you are light in
the Lord. Live as children of light (for the fruit of the
light consists in all goodness, righteousness and
truth) and find out what pleases the Lord. Have
nothing to do with the fruitless deeds of darkness,
but rather expose them. For it is shameful even to
mention what the disobedient do in secret. Be very
careful then, how you live — not as unwise but as
wise, making the most of every opportunity.

Ephesians 5:8–16

The Lord's Prayer

Our Father ...

Closing Prayer

Father of light and everlasting love, give us
through Christ our Lord the clarity to see your
will this day, the strength to follow it and the
fervour to love you, above all things, and our
neighbour for your sake. Amen.

A Selection of Midday Prayers

Teach us, good Lord, to serve you as you deserve; to give and not to count the cost; to fight and not to heed the wounds; to toil and not to seek for rest; to labour and not to ask for any reward, save that of knowing that we do your will; through Jesus Christ our Lord.

Saint Ignatius of Loyola

Lord Jesus, our Saviour, let us now come to you:
Our hearts are cold; Lord, warm them with your
    selfless love.
Our hearts are sinful; cleanse them with your
    precious blood.
Our hearts are weak; strengthen them with your
    joyous Spirit.

Our hearts are empty; fill them with your divine
    presence.
Lord Jesus, our hearts are yours; possess them always
    and only for yourself.

Saint Augustine of Hippo

Still am I haunting
Thy door with my prayers;
Still they are panting
Up thy steep stairs!
Wouldst thou not rather
Come down to my heart,
And there, O my Father,
Be what thou art?

George Macdonald

Almighty God, help us not to judge others by
appearances. Help us, Lord, to understand that no
matter what race or colour we are, or what age, we
are all equally your sons and daughters. May we

never intentionally and deliberately give hurt or
offence to anyone. Help us to realize that if we are
all your sons and daughters, that makes us brothers
and sisters in your family. We need your help to
understand this and live it out in our lives. Amen.

A. C.

Father, I look at Jesus and see what I long to be.
I am tired and I see in him your creative energy;
I care what people think of me, but Jesus went on
　　his way,
ready to be laughed at;
I miss so often the real longing in the words of my
　　friends,
but Jesus knows the heart;
I fear the future, but I see Jesus setting his face to go
　　up to Jerusalem.
Thank you, Father, for Jesus our brother,
revealing human nature as you created it to be,

and staying with us in all our days.

Bernard Thorogood

Teach us, O Spirit of God, that silent language
which says all things. Teach our souls to remain
silent in your presence: that we may adore you in
the depths of our being and await all things from
you, whilst asking of you nothing but the
accomplishment of your will. Teach us to remain
quiet under your action and produce in our soul
that deep and simple prayer which says nothing
and expresses everything, which specifies nothing
and expresses everything.

John Nicholas Grou

My Lord God,
I have no idea where I am going.
I do not see the road ahead of me.
I cannot know for certain where it will end.

Nor do I really know myself,
and the fact that I think that I am following
your will does not mean that I am
actually doing so.
But I believe that the desire to please you
does in fact please you.
And I hope I have that desire in all that I am doing.
I hope that I will never do anything apart from that
  desire.
And I know that if I do this,
you will lead me by the right road though I
may know nothing about it.
Therefore will I trust you always though I
may seem lost and in the shadow of death.
I will not fear, for you are ever with me,
and you will never leave me to face my perils alone.

Thomas Merton

Lord, it's just when we most need the light of your
love in our lives that we least feel like asking for it.

When things go wrong and life seems dismal and grey, be with us, Lord, to support and strengthen us. Help us never to give up hope, but to place all our trust in your love, confident that your Son will lift us up and fill our lives again with joy. Please hear our prayer through the same Christ our Lord. Amen.

A. C.

Evening Prayer: A Simple Pattern

Evening Prayer, also known as Vespers or Evensong, is one of the most ancient practices of the Christian Church. Along with Morning Prayer or Matins, it was introduced almost from the very beginning. This was in imitation of Jewish tradition at the time of Jesus. At the Reformation the English Church revised the pattern used by the monasteries for many hundreds of years, but retained the same basic structure. Here we have a simple form of that same traditional prayer of the Church.

Evening Prayer

Lord, open my lips,
and my mouth will proclaim your praise.

Glory be to the Father, and to the Son, and to the
Holy Spirit, as it was in the beginning, is now, and
ever shall be, world without end. Amen.

Poem

Christ be near at either hand,
Christ behind, before me stand,
Christ with me where'er I go,
Christ around, above, below.

Christ be in my heart and mind,
Christ within my soul enshrined,
Christ control my wayward heart;
Christ abide and ne'er depart.

Christ my life and only way,
Christ my lantern night and day:
Christ be my unchanging friend,
Guide and shepherd to the end.

The Psalms

Psalm 141:1–4

May my prayer rise up before you like incense.

O Lord, I call to you;
come quickly to me.
Hear my voice when I call to you.
May my prayer be set before you like incense;
may the lifting up of my hands
be like the evening sacrifice.

Set a guard over my mouth, O Lord;
keep watch over the door of my lips.
Let not my heart be drawn to what is evil,

to take part in wicked deeds
with those who are evildoers;
let me not share their feasting.

May my prayer rise up before you like incense.

Psalm 16:1–8
I will praise the Lord who counsels me.

Keep me safe, O God,
for in you I take refuge.

I said to the Lord, 'You are my God;
My happiness lies in you alone.'

As for the faithful who are in the land,
they are the glorious ones in whom is all my
    delight.

I will praise the Lord, who counsels me;
even at night my heart instructs me.

I have set the Lord always before me.
Because he is at my right hand, I shall not be shaken.

I will praise the Lord who counsels me.

Canticle

Philippians 2:6—11

Let every creature bend the knee at the name of Jesus.

Though he was in the form of God,
Jesus did not count equality with God a thing to be
     grasped.

He emptied himself
taking the very nature of a servant,

being made in human likeness.

And being found in appearance as a man,
he humbled himself and became obedient unto
    death,
even death on a cross.

Therefore God exalted him to the highest place
and gave him the name that is above every name,

That at the name of Jesus every knee should bow,
in heaven and on earth and under the earth,

And every tongue confess that Jesus Christ is Lord,
to the glory of God the Father.

**Let every creature bend the knee at the name of
Jesus.**

The Word of God

We have not stopped praying for you and asking
God to fill you with the knowledge of his will
through all spiritual wisdom and understanding.
And we pray this in order that you may live a life
worthy of the Lord and may please him in every
way: bearing fruit in every good work, growing in
the knowledge of God, being strengthened with all
power according to his glorious might so that you
may have great endurance and patience.

Colossians 1:9–11

The Canticle of Mary

Luke 1:46–53

My spirit rejoices in God my Saviour.

My soul glorifies the Lord
and my spirit rejoices in God my Saviour,

For he had been mindful
of the humble state of his servant.
From now on all generations will call me blessed,
for the Mighty One has done great things for me —
holy is his name.

His mercy extends to those who fear him,
from generation to generation.

He has performed mighty deeds with his arm;
he has scattered those who are proud in their
    inmost thoughts.

He has brought down rulers from their thrones,
but has lifted up the humble.
He has filled the hungry with good things
but has sent the rich away empty.

My spirit rejoices in God my Saviour.

Prayers of Intercession

To be used as a basis for your own intercession.

Our God is a loving Father who cares for us and
knows every one of our needs. With confidence
we pray:
Father, may we find rest in your love.

Christ, your Son, knew suffering and the last hours
of death; be with all who, as we pray, are suffering
and near to death.
Father, may we find rest in your love.

Christ, your Son, knew loneliness and betrayal; be
with all who, this evening, are in despair and feel
unattractive, useless and unloved.
Father, may we find rest in your love.

Christ, your Son, was at the beck and call of many in

need; be with doctors, nurses, and carers of all kinds
who continue your Son's work of loving service.
Father, may we find rest in your love.

Christ, your Son, left us the Spirit of his love; be
with us as we learn to care for those who we find
irritating and unappreciative of our efforts.
Father, may we find rest in your love.

Closing Prayer

Father, learning from the example
of Christ Jesus, your Son, teach us to love
without counting the cost or seeking any reward;
may we seek to love others,
as you generously love us. Amen.
May the Lord bless us,
may he keep us from all evil
and lead us to life everlasting. Amen.

A Selection of Evening and Night Prayers

Dear God, you are always surprising me.
My day was just a few hours of life,
yet in it you were teaching me new things.
You showed me a fresh aspect of familiar people I met,
and new truth about myself.
Forgive my slowness to understand your word;
don't add up the wasted minutes;
judge all my work with a father's mercy.
Thank you, Lord, for the light and the night;
enable me to find renewal in sleep,
and let me know, deep in my heart,
that tomorrow I will be with you, through Jesus
    Christ.

Bernard Thorogood

Forgive me, O God,

    For the time I have wasted today;

    For the people I have hurt today;

    For the tasks I have shirked today.

Help me

    Not to be discouraged when things are difficult;

    Not to be content with second bests;

    To do better tomorrow than I have done today.

And help me always to remember that Jesus is with
me and that I am not trying all alone.

This I ask for Jesus' sake. Amen.

William Barclay

Holy Spirit, I thank you for the quiet moments of
this busy day when you spoke to me of your abiding
love. Teach me now as I lie down to rest how to
listen to you when you speak in the silence of the
night, in the silence of my heart. Teach me waking

or sleeping how to watch and how to listen for your
still, small voice which gives meaning and direction
to every moment of my life.

Michael Buckley

Holy Spirit, I thank you for being with me
this day, for all the happiness your will has
brought, and for all the toil and hardships I have
had to accept. Forgive me for the times when I
have forgotten you amid the cares of life. Forgive
me also if I have not accepted any suffering in the
same spirit as Christ my Lord. Help me to rest in
peace this night, that I may wake truly refreshed
and willing to spend a new day in your service.
Guard me this night, as the good shepherd
guards his flock. Grant that, in your mercy and
love, when I close my eyes on this world for
the last time, I may wake in the joy of your
presence to a new everlasting day.

Harold Winstone

Most Holy Trinity, I commit my life, as I do this day, now drawing to a close, to your infinite mercy, trust and love. For my lack of faith I ask mercy of the Father, who is swift to compassion and slow to anger; for my inability to trust your providence, I seek refuge in the humanity of the Son who was obedient unto death; for my coldness in loving, I place myself in the warmth of the Holy Spirit who alone makes our lives acceptable to you. May this night's repose refresh my body and soul so that tomorrow's dawn may find me more ready to give glory to the Father, Son and Holy Spirit.

Michael Buckley

O Lord our God, what sins I have this day committed in word, deed, or thought, forgive me, for you are gracious, and you love everyone. Grant me peaceful and undisturbed sleep, send me your guardian angel to protect and guard me from

every evil, for you are the guardian of our souls
and bodies, and to you we ascribe glory, to the
Father and the Son and the Holy Ghost, now and
for ever and unto the ages of ages.

Russian Orthodox Prayer

O Lord my God, thank you
    for bringing this day to a close;
Thank you for giving me this rest
    in body and soul.
Your hand has been over me
    and has guarded and preserved me.
Forgive my lack of faith
    and any wrong that I have done today,
    and help me to forgive all who have wronged
    me.
Let me sleep in peace under your protection,
    and keep me from all the temptations of
    darkness.
Into your hands I commend my loved ones

and all who dwell in this house;
I commend to you my body and soul.
O God, your holy name be praised.

Dietrich Bonhoeffer

Night Prayer:
A Simple Pattern

Night, for the Christian, has always been symbolic of death. As Jesus hung dying upon the cross, 'darkness came over the whole land' (Luke 23:44).

Sleep can seem so like death that parents tiptoe into bedrooms and hang, breathless, over cots to check that their child still breathes. In our cities the elderly and vulnerable will not venture out after dark. For them 'the pestilence that stalks in the darkness' is only too real. They need to be reassured that 'the Lord is my refuge'.

Since the development of Compline, or Night Prayer, in the fourth century, Christians have commended themselves last thing at night into the loving hands of God. Traditionally, Night Prayer com- mences with a reflective review of the day,

especially of any failures to live up to the ideals
of Christ.

Night Prayer

The Psalm

Psalm 91:1–4

He is my refuge; my God, in whom I trust.

He who dwells in the shelter of the Most High
will rest in the shadow of the Almighty.
I will say of the Lord, 'He is my refuge and
 my fortress,
my God, in whom I trust.'

Surely he will save you from the fowler's snare
and from the deadly pestilence.
He will cover you with his feathers,

and under his wings you will find refuge;
his faithfulness will be your shield and rampart.

He is my refuge; my God, in whom I trust.

The Word of God

May God himself, the God of peace, sanctify you
through and through. May your whole spirit, soul
and body be kept blameless at the coming of our
Lord Jesus Christ.

1 Thessalonians 5:23

The Canticle of Simeon

Luke 2:29–32

Lord, save us while we are awake;
protect us while we sleep.

Now, Lord, you have kept your word:

let your servant go in peace.

With my own eyes I have seen the salvation
which you have prepared in the sight of every
    people:

A light to reveal you to the nations
and the glory of your people Israel.

**Lord, save us while we are awake;
protect us while we sleep.**

Closing Prayer

Lord, Faithful and True,
give our bodies restful sleep;
and may all that we have done today
in work and leisure
give you glory and praise. Amen.

Alternative Poems, Hymns and Prayers

Advent

Come, my Way, my Truth, my Life:
Such a Way, as gives us breath:
Such a Truth, as ends all strife:
Such a Life, as killeth death.

Come, my Light, my Feast, my Strength:
Such a Light, as shows a feast:
Such a Feast, as mends in length:
Such a Strength, as makes his guest.

Come, my Joy, my Love, my Heart:
Such a Joy, as none can move:

Such a Love, as none can part:
Such a Heart, as joys in Love.

George Herbert

Let me love thee, O Christ,
   in thy first coming,
when thou wast made a man, for love of men,
   and for love of me.

Let me love thee, O Christ,
   in thy second coming,
when with an inconceivable love
thou standest and knockest at the door,
and wouldst enter into the souls of men,
   and into mine.

Plant in my soul, O Christ, thy likeness of love;
   that when by death thou callest,
it may be ready

and burning
    to come unto thee.

Eric Milner-White

Prayer for Advent

Lord,
to free humankind from its sinful state
you sent your only Son into this world.
Grant to us who, in faith and love, wait for his coming
your gift of grace
and the reward of true freedom. Amen.

Christmas

On Christmas night all Christians sing
To hear the news the angels bring –
News of great joy, news of great mirth,
News of our merciful King's birth.

Then why should men on earth be sad,
Since our Redeemer made us glad,
When from our sins he set us free,
All for to gain our liberty?

When sin departs before his grace,
Then life and health come in its place;
Angels and men with joy may sing,
All for to see the new-born King.

All out of darkness we have light,
Which made the angels sing this night:
'Glory to God and peace to men,
Now and for evermore. Amen.'

Traditional

I sing of a maiden
That is makèless;
King of all kings
To her son she ches.

He came all so still
Where his mother was,
As dew in April
That falleth on the grass.

He came all so still
To his mother's bowr,
As dew in April
That falleth on the flower.

He came all so still
There his mother lay,
As dew in April
That falleth on the spray.

Mother and maiden
Was never none but she;
Well may such a lady
Godes mother be.

*This 15th century Christmas poem by
an unknown writer is from the Sloane MS.
'Makèless' means 'matchless', and 'ches' means 'chose'.*

Prayer for Christmas

Almighty and Infinite God,
your Incarnate Word fills us
with the new light he brought to humankind.
Let the light of faith in our hearts shine
through everything that we do and say.
We make this prayer through Christ our Lord.
    Amen.

Lent

Lead, kindly light, amid the encircling gloom,
    Lead thou me on;
The night is dark, and I am far from home,
    Lead thou me on.
Keep thou my feet: I do not ask to see
The distant scene; one step enough for me.

I was not ever thus, nor prayed that thou
    Shouldst lead me on;
I loved to choose and see my path; but now
    Lead thou me on.
I loved the garish day, and, spite of fears,
Pride ruled my will: remember not past
    years.

So long thy power hath blest me, sure it still
    Will lead me on,
O'er moor and fen, o'er crag and torrent, till

The night is gone,
And with the morn those angel faces smile,
Which I have loved long since, and lost awhile.

John H. Newman

The royal feast was done; the king
Sought some new sport to banish care,
And to his jester cried: 'Sir Fool,
Kneel now, and make for us a prayer!'

The jester doffed his cap and bells,
And stood the mocking court before;
They could not see the bitter smile
Behind the painted grin he wore.

He bowed his head, and bent his knee
Upon the monarch's silken stool;
His pleading voice arose: 'O Lord,
Be merciful to me, a fool!

'Tis not by guilt the onward sweep
of truth and right, O Lord, we stay;
'Tis by our follies that so long
We hold the earth from heaven away.

These clumsy feet, still in the mire,
Go crushing blossoms without end;
These hard, well-meaning hands we thrust
Among the heart-strings of a friend.

The ill-timed truth we might have kept —
Who knows how sharp it pierced and stung!
The word we had not sense to say —
Who knows how gladly it had rung!

Our faults no tenderness should ask,
The chastening stripes must cleanse them all;
But for our blunders — O, in shame
Before the eyes of heaven we fail.

Earth bears no balsam for mistakes;
Men crown the knave and scourge the tool
That did his will; but thou, O Lord,
Be merciful to me, a fool!'

The room was hushed; in silence rose
the king, and sought his gardens cool,
And walked apart, and murmured low,
'Be merciful to me, a fool!'

Rowland Hill

Magdalen at Michael's gate
Tirled at the pin;
On Joseph's thorn sang the blackbird,
'Let her in! Let her in!'

'Hast thou seen the wounds?' said Michael:
'Know'st thou thy sin?'
'It is evening, evening,' sang the blackbird,
'Let her in! Let her in!'

'Yes, I have seen the wounds,
And I know my sin.'
'She knows it well, well, well,' sang the blackbird,
'Let her in! Let her in!'

'Thou bringest no offerings?' said Michael.
'Nought save sin.'
And the blackbird sang, 'She is sorry, sorry, sorry.
Let her in! Let her in!'

When he had sung himself to sleep,
And night did begin,
One came and open'd Michael's gate,
And Magdalen went in.

Henry Kingsley

Prayer for Lent

Turn our hearts back to you, God our Saviour;
help us to acknowledge how we miss the mark
and sin.
Form us by your heavenly teaching,
so that we may truly profit
by our observance of Lent.
We make our prayer through Christ our Lord.
   Amen.

Easter

Bring, all ye dear-bought nations, bring,
Your richest praises to your king, alleluia,
that spotless Lamb, who more than due,
Paid for his sheep, and those sheep you, alleluia.
Alleluia, alleluia, alleluia.

That guiltless Son, who bought your peace,
And made his Father's anger cease, alleluia.
Then, Life and Death together fought,
Each to a strange extreme were brought, alleluia.
Alleluia, alleluia, alleluia.

We, Lord, with faithful hearts and voice,
On this thy rising day rejoice, alleluia.
O thou, whose power o'ercame the grave,
By grace and love us sinners save, alleluia.
Alleluia, alleluia, alleluia.

Wipo (Eleventh Century)

Now the green blade riseth
　　from the buried grain,
wheat that in the dark earth
　　many days has lain;
love lives again,
　　that with the dead has been:
love is come again
　　like wheat that springeth green.

In the grave they laid him,
   Love whom men had slain,
thinking that never
   he would wake again,
laid in the earth
   like grain that sleeps unseen:
love is come again
   like wheat that springeth green.

Forth he came at Easter,
   like the risen grain,
he that for three days
   in the grave had lain;
quick from the dead
   my risen Lord is seen;
love is come again
   like wheat that springeth green.

When our hearts are wintry,
   grieving or in pain,

thy touch can call us
    back to life again,
fields of our heart
    that dead and bare have been:
love is come again
    like wheat that springeth green.

J. M. C. Crum

Prayer for Easter

At this season, Lord God,
you opened for us the way to eternal life
through your only Son's victory over death.
Grant that as we celebrate the feast
of his glorious resurrection
we may be renewed by your Holy Spirit
and, in our own lives, rise up again to
a freshness and vigour of loving service and praise.
    Amen.

Pentecost

Come down, O love divine,
seek thou this soul of mine,
and visit it with thine own
    ardour glowing;
O comforter, draw near,
within my heart appear,
and kindle it, thy holy
    flame bestowing.

O let it freely burn,
till earthly passions turn
to dust and ashes in its
    heat consuming;
and let thy glorious light
shine ever on my sight,
and clothe me round, the while
    my path illuming.

Let holy charity
mine outward vesture be,
and lowliness become mine
    inner clothing;
true lowliness of heart,
which takes the humbler part,
and o'er its own shortcomings
    weeps with loathing.

And so the yearning strong,
with which the soul will long,
shall far outpass the power of
    human telling;
for none can guess its grace,
till he become the place
wherein the Holy Spirit makes
    his dwelling.

Bianco da Siena

Prayer for Pentecost

Lord Spirit,
you have enlivened our darkened world
with the gift of your life, light and love;
lead us unfalteringly to open the eyes of the blind,
and proclaim Christ's Good News of love,
to the glory of the Father, the Son
and the Holy Spirit. Amen.

Alternative Psalms
and Readings

The weekly cycles of psalms and readings given here
are appropriate for use at any time of day.

Alternative Psalms

Sunday

Psalm 1:1–3,6

**The Lord watches over the way of the
righteous.**

Blessed is the man
who does not walk in the counsel of the wicked
or stand in the way of sinners

or sit in the seat of mockers.

But his delight is in the law of the Lord,
and on his law he mediates day and night.

He is like a tree planted by streams of water,
which yields its fruit in season
and whose leaf does not wither.
Whatever he does prospers.

For the Lord watches over the way of the
    righteous,
but the way of the wicked will perish.

**The Lord watches over the way of the
    righteous.**

Monday

Psalm 8:1,3–9

O Lord how majestic is your name.

O Lord, our Lord,
how majestic is your name in all the earth!
You have set your glory above the heavens.

When I consider your heavens,
the work of your fingers,
the moon and the stars,
which you have set in place,
what is man that you are mindful of him,
the son of man that you care for him?

You made him a little lower than the heavenly
    beings
and crowned him with glory and honour.

You made him ruler over the works of your hands;
you put everything under his feet:

all flocks and herds,
and the beasts of the field,
the birds of the air,
and the fish of the sea,
all that swim the paths of the seas.

O Lord, our Lord, how majestic is your name
in all the earth!

O Lord, how majestic is your name.

Tuesday

Psalm 13:1–3,5–6

I trust in your unfailing love.

How long, O Lord? Will you forget me forever?

How long will you hide your face from me?

How long must I wrestle with my thoughts
and every day have sorrow in my heart?
How long will my enemy triumph over me?

Look on me and answer, O Lord my God.
Give light to my eyes, or I will sleep in death.

But I trust in your unfailing love;
my heart rejoices in your salvation.
I will sing to the Lord,
for he has been good to me.

I trust in your unfailing love.

Wednesday

Psalm 40:1–3

Blessed is the man who makes the Lord his trust.

I waited patiently for the Lord;
he turned to me and heard my cry.

He lifted me out of the slimy pit,
out of the mud and mire;

He set my feet on a rock
and gave me a firm place to stand.

He put a new song in my mouth,
a hymn of praise to our God.

Many will see and fear,
and put their trust in the Lord.

Blessed is the man who makes the Lord his trust.

Thursday

Psalm 136:1–5,23–26

Give thanks to the Lord.

Give thanks to the Lord, for he is good.
His love endures forever.
Give thanks to the God of gods.
His love endures for ever.
Give thanks to the Lord of lords:
His love endures for ever.
to him who alone does great wonders,
His love endures for ever.
who by his understanding made the heavens,
His love endures for ever.
to the One who remembered us in our estate
His love endures for ever.
and freed us from our enemies,
His love endures for ever.

and who gives food to every creature.

His love endures for ever.

Give thanks to the God of heaven.

His love endures for ever.

Give thanks to the Lord.

Friday

Psalm 90:1–2,12,14,17

Establish the work of our hands.

Lord, you have been our dwelling place
throughout all generations.
Before the mountains were born
or you brought forth the earth and the world,
from everlasting to everlasting you are God.

Teach us to number our days aright,
that we may gain a heart of wisdom.

Satisfy us in the morning with your unfailing love,
that we may sing for joy and be glad all our days.

May the favour of the Lord our God rest upon us;
establish the work of our hands for us —
yes, establish the work of our hands.

Establish the work of our hands.

Saturday

Psalm 139:1–4,7–8,13–14
Search me, O God, and know my heart.

O Lord, you have searched me
and you know me.
You know when I sit and when I rise;
you perceive my thoughts from afar.

You discern my going out and my lying down;
you are familiar with all my ways.
Before a word is on my tongue
you know it completely, O Lord.

Where can I go from your Spirit?
Where can I flee from your presence?
If I go up to the heavens, you are there;
if I make my bed in the depths, you are there.

For you created my inmost being;
you knit me together in my mother's womb.
I praise you because I am fearfully
and wonderfully made;
your works are wonderful,
I know that full well.

Search me, O God, and know my heart.

Alternative Readings

Sunday

After the Sabbath, at dawn on the first day of the week, Mary Magdalene and the other Mary went to look at the tomb.

There was a violent earthquake, for an angel of the Lord came down from heaven and, going to the tomb, rolled back the stone and sat on it. His appearance was like lightning, and his clothes were white as snow. The guards were so afraid of him that they shook and became like dead men.

The angel said to the women, 'Do not be afraid, for I know that you are looking for Jesus, who was crucified. He is not here; he has risen, just as he said.'

Matthew 28:1–6

Monday

Do not let any unwholesome talk come out of your mouths, but only what is helpful for building others up according to their needs, that it may benefit those who listen. And do not grieve the Holy Spirit of God, with whom you were sealed for the day of redemption. Get rid of all bitterness, rage and anger, brawling and slander, along with every form of malice. Be kind and compassionate to one another, forgiving each other, just as in Christ God forgave you.

Ephesians 4:29–32

Tuesday

Oh, the depth of the riches of the wisdom and
    knowledge of God.
How unsearchable his judgements,
and his paths beyond tracing out!

'Who has known the mind of the Lord?
'Or who has been his counsellor?'
'Who has ever given to God,
that God should repay him?'
For from him and through him and to him are
    all things.
To him be the glory for ever! Amen.

Romans 11:33–36

Wednesday

The kingdom of God does not mean food and drink
but righteousness and peace and joy in the Holy
Spirit; he who thus serves Christ is acceptable to
God and approved by men. Let us then pursue what
makes for peace and for mutual upbuilding.

Romans 14:17–19

Thursday

Everyone should be quick to listen, slow to speak and slow to become angry, for man's anger does not bring about the righteous life that God desires. Therefore, get rid of all moral filth and the evil that is so prevalent, and humbly accept the word planted in you, which can save you.

Do not merely listen to the word, and so deceive yourselves. Do what it says. The man who looks intently into the perfect law that gives freedom and continues to do this, not forgetting what he has heard, but doing it — he will be blessed in what he does.

James 1:19–22,25

Friday

Who shall separate us from the love of Christ? Shall trouble or hardship or persecution or famine or

nakedness or danger or sword? No, in all these
things we are more than conquerors through him
who loved us.

Romans 8:35–37

Saturday

Love must be sincere. Hate what is evil; cling to what
is good. Be devoted to one another in brotherly love.
Honour one another above yourselves. Never be
lacking in zeal, but keep your spiritual fervour,
serving the Lord. Be joyful in hope, patient in
affliction, faithful in prayer.

Romans 12:9–12

Occasional Prayers

Table Prayers

We thank and praise you, Lord, for the gifts of your
creation, and ask your blessing on mankind that one
day we can learn to share with poorer nations so
that no one will go hungry. We ask this through
Jesus Christ our Lord. Amen.

Delia Smith

We thank you, Father, for the holy resurrection,
which you made known to us through Jesus, your
Child. As the ingredients of the bread on this table,
though once separate, were gathered together and
made one, so may your Church be built up from
the ends of the earth and gathered into your
kingdom; for power and glory are yours through

all the endless succession of ages. Amen.

Pseudo-Athanasius

O Lord our God, you are the Bread that is eaten in heaven, the Bread that gives life, the Food that really nourishes the whole world. You came down from heaven and gave the world life; you guide us through this present existence, and you have promised that there will be another for us to enjoy after this. Bless, then, our food and drink and enable us to take them without sinning. May we receive them thankfully and give you glory for them, for you it is who confers all good gifts upon us. Blessed and glorious is your name, ever worthy of honour.

Third Century Prayer

For the Family

We thank you, Father, for the gift of Jesus your Son
who came to our earth and lived in a simple home.
We have a greater appreciation of the value and
dignity of the human family because he loved and
was loved within its shelter. Bless us this day; may
we grow in love for each other in our family and so
give thanks to you who are the maker of all human
families and our abiding peace.

Michael Buckley

Almighty God and heavenly Father, we thank you
for the children whom you have given to us; give us
also grace to train them in your faith, fear and love;
that as they advance in years they may grow in
grace, and be found hereafter in the number of your
elect children; through Jesus Christ our Lord.

John Cosin

Lord, I want above all to bring up my children to know and love you. It is not easy to explain to them that you love them and care for them, especially when things go wrong and they are hurt physically or wounded mentally. I know I must show my trust in you and go on serenely and lovingly when I too am hurt. Take me over, Lord, completely, rule my life and shine through me with your light so that they may know that you are a living and loving God. Please let me forget myself through loving you, for this is the way that they will grow to see the depth of your love. Help me dear Lord.

Michael Hollings and Etta Gullick

O Lord Jesus, be near to all young children, that in the peril and confusion of this age their growing spirits may take no hurt at our hands, and grant to parents such sure knowledge of your love that they may guide their children with courage and faith.

New Every Morning

Dear Lord, who has blessed us with the gift of family life, that we may learn to love and care for others: We praise you for the example of your Son Jesus Christ, who even when deserted and betrayed by closest friends took thought for his mother and his disciple. Open our eyes to recognize in all men the claims of kinship, and stir our hearts to serve them as brethren called with us into the sonship of your love.

Basil Naylor

God our Father, we pray for our young people growing up in an unstable and confusing world.

Show them that your ways give more meaning to

life than the ways of the world, and that following you is better than chasing after selfish goals.

Help them to take failure not as a measure of their worth but as a chance for a new start.

Give them strength to hold their faith in you, and to keep alive their joy in your creation; through Jesus Christ our Lord.

Episcopal Church, USA

For Friends

Lord Jesus, you had friends and felt lonely and abandoned when at the end of your life, they left you to suffer alone. Help us to be good friends, loyal and reliable, ready to help whenever we can. While we have special friends, please help us to be friendly with everyone, remembering that you asked us to love one another as you have loved us. Amen.

A. C.

May the God of love
who is the source of all our affection
for each other formed here on earth
take our friendships into his keeping,
that they may continue and increase
throughout life and beyond it,
in Jesus Christ our Lord.

William Temple

I thank you for my friends,
For those who understand me better than I
    understand myself,
For those who know me at my worst and still
    like me,
For those who have forgiven me when I had no
    right to expect to be forgiven.
Help me to be as true to my friends as I would wish
    them to be to me.

William Barclay

'Before' Prayers

Before Reading Scripture

Eternal Light, shine into our hearts;
Eternal Goodness, deliver us from evil
Eternal Power, be our support;
Eternal Wisdom, scatter the darkness of our
    ignorance;
Eternal Pity, have mercy upon us;
that with all our heart and mind and soul and
    strength we may seek your face and be brought
    by your infinite mercy to your holy presence;
    through Jesus Christ our Lord.

Alcuin

O Lord, you have given us your word for a light to
shine upon our path; grant us so to meditate on that
word, and to follow its teaching, that we may find in
it the light that shines more and more until the

perfect day; through Jesus Christ our Lord.

Saint Jerome

Let us keep the Scriptures in mind and meditate
upon them day and night, persevering in prayer,
always on the watch. Let us beg the Lord to give us
real knowledge of what we read and to show us not
only how to understand it but how to put it into
practice, so that we may deserve to obtain spiritual
grace, enlightened by the law of the Holy Spirit,
through Jesus Christ our Lord, whose power and
glory will endure throughout the ages. Amen.

Origen

Before Study

Lord,
Grant us the knowledge that we need
To solve the questions of the mind;
Light our candles while we read,

To keep our hearts from going blind;
Enlarge our vision to behold
The wonders you have worked of old;
Reveal yourself in every law,
And gild the towers of truth with holy awe.

Henry van Dyke

God of Truth, who has guided men in knowledge throughout the ages, and from whom every good thought comes, help us in our study to use your gifts of wisdom and knowledge. Let us read good books carefully, and listen to all wise teaching humbly that we may be led into all truth, and strengthened in all the goodness of life, to the praise of your holy name. Amen.

Rowland Williams

Before Worship

Holy Spirit, you make alive;
bless also this our gathering,
the speaker and the hearer;
fresh from the heart it shall come,
by your aid,
let it also go to the heart.

Søren Kierkegaard

Eternal God, we come, we come again,
seeking, hoping, wanting to hear your word.

We come because, despite our best efforts,
we have failed to live by bread alone.

We come impelled by a desire too deep for
    words,
with longings that are too infinite to express.

95

We come yearning for meaning in our existence
and purpose for our life.

We come acknowledging our need for each other's
affirmation and encouragement, understanding and
   love.

We come confessing our dependence on you.
Lord, embrace us with your forgiveness, and claim us
by the mystery and depths of your love. Amen.

Terry Falla

O God, the world is so much with me, late and soon.
Every day brings its tasks, its trials, its temptations.
I may sometimes resent the rush and clamour of
everyday life; but if the world was suddenly to be
stilled, to an unbroken and deathly silence, I should
be distressed far more.

   I am glad, though, for the stillness of Sunday
morning; for the anticipation of the day's work and

worship; for the chance it will give of rich enjoyment, true recreation, of body, mind and spirit; for the so welcome change from the everyday run of things.

Leonard Barnett

In Thanksgiving

Lord Jesus, I thank you
not just with my lips and heart
but with my spirit, with which I recognize
and love you.
You are my all, and everything is in you.
In you I live, move and have being.

You are my brother, my all.
You are the true God, the true Son of God
to whom all honour, glory and thanks
are due.

Gallican Formularies

Giver of all good things, we thank you: for health
and vigour; for the air that gives the breath of life,
the sun that warms us, and the good food that
makes us strong; for happy homes and for the
friends we love; for all that makes it good to live.
Make us thankful and eager to repay, by
cheerfulness and kindliness, and by a readiness to
help others. Freely we have received; let us freely
give, in the name of him who gave his life for us,
Jesus Christ our Lord.

Thomas Ken

My God, from my heart I thank you for the many
blessings you have given me. I thank you for having
created and baptized me, for having placed me in
your holy Church, and for having given me so many
graces and mercies through the merits of Jesus
Christ. I thank your Son Jesus, for having died upon
the cross that I might receive pardon for my sins and

obtain my eternal salvation. I thank you for all your other mercies you have given me through Jesus Christ, Our Lord.

Michael Buckley

Seeking God's Will

You have placed the honour of your will in my hands. Each word of your revelation says that you respect and trust me, that you give me dignity and responsibility. Teach me to understand that. Give me that holy maturity that is capable of receiving the light you grant and of assuming the responsibility that you entrust. Keep my heart awake that at all times it may be before you, and let what I do become one with the command and the obedience to which you have called me.

Romano Guardini

Dear Lord, quieten my spirit and fix my thoughts on
your will, that I may see what you have done, and
contemplate its doing without self-consciousness or
inner excitement, without haste and without delay,
without fear of other people's judgements or
anxiety about success, knowing only that it is your
will and therefore must be done quietly, faithfully
and lovingly, for in your will alone is our peace.

George Appleton

Almighty God, in whom we live and move and have
our being, you have made us for yourself, so that
our hearts are restless until they rest in you; grant us
purity of heart and strength of purpose, that no
selfish passion may hinder us from knowing your
will, no weakness from doing it; but that in your
light we may see light clearly, and in your service
find our perfect freedom; through Jesus Christ our
Lord.

Saint Augustine of Hippo

For Peace

Lord, make me an instrument of your peace;
where there is hatred let me sow love,
where there is injury let me sow pardon,
where there is doubt let me sow faith,
where there is despair let me give hope,
where there is darkness let me give light,
where there is sadness let me give joy.
O divine master, grant that I may
not try to be comforted but to comfort,
not try to be understood but to understand,
not try to be loved but to love.

Because it is in giving that we receive,
it is in forgiving that we are forgiven,
and it is in dying that we are born to eternal life.

Unknown Source
(Attributed to Saint Francis of Assisi, but first appeared in 1913)

O Lord, calm the waves of this heart; calm its tempest! Calm thyself, O my soul, so that the divine can act in thee! Calm thyself, O my soul, so that God is able to repose in thee, so that his peace may cover thee! Yes, Father in heaven, often have we found that the world cannot give us peace. O but make us feel that thou art able to give peace; let us know the truth of thy promise: that the whole world may not be able to take away thy peace.

Søren Kierkegaard

Deep peace of the Running Wave to you.
Deep peace of the Flowing Air to you.
Deep peace of the Quiet Earth to you.
Deep peace of the Shining Stars to you.
Deep peace of the Son of Peace to you.

Celtic Benediction

In Sickness and Distress

Lord, let this sickness, like that of Lazarus, be unto the Father's glory and for the good of those who stand by. I must see to it that whatever I have to suffer is not wasted but is offered to the Father, and also that I do not give cause for disedification to those who have to wait on me. Inspire me during my illness at least to think of you occasionally: I do not want to make this time, so far as prayer is concerned, a blank. If my regular practices have to be abandoned, show me what new ones I may substitute. Give me, I pray you, a more vivid awareness of your presence, so as to make up for the kind of willed recollection which I try to maintain when I am well.

Hubert van Zeller

Grant, Lord, that as you sent this sickness to me, you
will also send your Holy Spirit into my heart so that
my present illness may be sanctified and used as a
school in which I may learn to know the greatness
of my misery and the riches of your mercy. May I be
so humbled at my misery that I despair not of your
mercy and thus renounce all confidence in myself
and every other creature so that I may put the
whole of my salvation in your all-sufficient merits.

Lewis Bayley

For the Sick and the Dying

O God the Creator and Father of all,
We praise you that your will is life
    and health and strength.
Help all who are ill or in pain
    to place themselves in your hands
        in loving trust,

so that your healing life may flow into them
    to make them well and strong,
    able and ready to do your holy will;
through him who has made known to us
    both your love and your will,
even Jesus Christ our Lord.

George Appleton

O Saviour of the world, lifted upon the cross that all men might be drawn to your love, dying for the salvation of us all, we implore you to make that love and that salvation a growing reality of glory to those who face their death. Grant to them, O Lord, your gift of a perfect repentance, and then may the heaven of your forgiveness banish all fears from them forever.

Elizabeth Goudge

Father,
you made us in your image
and your Son accepted death for our salvation.
Help those who are now, at this moment,
at the point of leaving this life.
May they be free of pain and distress
and may their parting be in dignity
accompanied by a knowledge of your love
and the love of their families.

A. C.

For Those who Mourn

We seem to give them back to thee, O God, who gavest them to us. Yet as thou didst not lose them in giving, so we do not lose them by their return. Not as the world giveth, givest thou, O lover of souls. What thou givest, thou takest not away, for what is thine is ours also if we are thine. And life is eternal and love is immortal, and death is only an horizon, and an horizon is nothing save the limit of our sight. Lift us up, strong Son of God, that we may see further; cleanse our eyes that we may see more clearly: draw us closer to thyself that we may know ourselves to be nearer to our loved ones who are with thee. And while thou dost prepare a place for us, prepare us also for that happy place, that where thou art we may be also for evermore. Amen.

Bede Jarrett

Grant, O Lord, to all who are bereaved, the spirit of faith and courage, that they may have the strength to meet the days to come with steadfastness and patience; not sorrowing as those without hope, but in thankful remembrance of your great goodness in past years, and in the sure expectation of a joyful reunion in the heavenly places; and this we ask in the name of Jesus Christ our Lord.

Irish Prayer Book

We remember, Lord, the slenderness of the
thread which separates life from death, and the
suddenness with which it can be broken. Help us
also to remember that on both sides of that division
we are surrounded by your love.

Persuade our hearts that when our dear ones die
neither we nor they are parted from you.

In you may we find peace, and in you be united
with them in the body of Christ, who has burst the
bonds of death and is alive for evermore, our Saviour
and theirs for ever and ever.

Dick Williams

For the Hungry

Make us worthy, Lord, to serve our fellow men
throughout the world who live and die in
poverty and hunger. Give them through our hands

this day their daily bread, and by our
understanding love, give peace and joy.

Mother Teresa of Calcutta

O God our Father, in the name of him who gave
bread to the hungry we remember all who, through
our human ignorance, folly, selfishness and sin, are
condemned to live in want; and we pray that all
endeavours for the overcoming of world poverty
and hunger may be so prospered that there may be
found food sufficient for all. We ask this through
Jesus Christ our Lord.

Christian Aid

Father, we deplore that in so rich a world we
tolerate poverty so harsh that men and women are
embittered by it, and children die or survive,
deprived in body, mind and spirit. Forgive our
ignorance, our indifference, and our unwillingness
to give the right priority to this responsibility. As we

have the knowledge by which we can produce more
than we need, stir up the compassion of us all by all
means possible, and give us the will and the wisdom,
that through political decisions, trade agreements,
and personal service, we may find the way to share
the wealth of the world, for the sake of him who
was prepared to become poor that we might be rich,
Jesus Christ our Lord.

CAFOD

For the Unemployed

Heavenly Father, who wills that every individual
should belong to the human community, look
with compassion on those who suffer distress
through lack of work; take from them the feeling
of rejection. Grant that they be free from want
and insecurity and may they soon find
employment, as those in the Gospel story who

were called at the eleventh hour to labour in
the vineyard, through Jesus Christ, our Lord.
Amen.

Michael Buckley

God our Father,
through and by the work of our hands
your mighty work of creation continues.
Hear the prayers of your people
and give all who seek employment
the opportunity to enhance their human dignity
and draw closer to one another
in mutual interdependence.

A. C.

For Those in Authority

O righteous Lord, may your Holy Spirit be with our
rulers, with our sovereign and all in authority under

her, that they may govern in your faith and fear, striving to put down all that is evil and to encourage all that is good. Give your spirit of wisdom to those who make our laws, grant that they may understand how great a work you have given them to do; that they may not do it lightly, but gravely and soberly, to the putting away of all wrong and oppression and to the advancement of the true welfare of your people.

Thomas Arnold

Grant, O God, and continue to give us a succession of legislators and rulers who have been taught the wisdom of the kingdom of Christ. Endow all members of Parliament with a right understanding, a pure purpose, and sound speech; enable them to rise above all self-seeking and party zeal into the larger sentiments of public good and human brotherhood. Purge our political life of every evil; subdue in the nation all unhallowed thirst for

conquest or vainglory. Inspire us with calmness and
self-restraint and the endeavour to get your will
done everywhere upon the earth.

John Hunter

Pour your blessing, O God, we pray you,
upon *Elizabeth our Queen*, that *she* may fulfil *her*
    calling as a Christian ruler.
Support *her* in the ceaseless round of duty,
inspire *her* in the service of many peoples.
Give *her* wise and selfless ministers,
bless *her* in home and family
and grant that, through *her*, the Commonwealth
may be knit together in one great brotherhood,
a strength and joy to all its members
and an instrument of peace in our troubled world,
through Jesus Christ, our Lord.

George Appleton

Acknowledgements

The compiler and publisher wish to express their gratitude to the following for the use of material of which they are the publisher, author or copyright holder:

Scripture quotations from the Holy Bible, New International Version, Copyright © 1973, 1978, 1984 by the International Bible Society, used by permission of Hodder and Stoughton Limited. All rights reserved. 'NIV' is a registered trademark of International Bible Society. US trademark number 1448790.

Hodder and Stoughton Limited for a prayer by Leonard Barnett from *A New Prayer Diary* and a prayer by Delia Smith from *A Book of Graces*.

SCM Press for a prayer by Dietrich Bonhoeffer from

his *Letters and Papers from Prison*.

The International Bible Reading Association for the prayers of Bernard Thorogood.

Fount Paperbacks (an imprint of HarperCollins*Publishers*) for the prayers by William Barclay from *A Plain Man's Book of Prayers*; and a poem by Teilhard de Chardin from *Le Milieu Divin*, first published in 1957 by Editions du Seuil.

The Society for Promoting Christian Knowledge for a prayer by Eric Milner-White from *My God, My Glory*; and the prayers of George Appleton from *One Man's Prayers*.

Monsignor Michael Buckley for his prayers from the compilation *The Treasury of the Holy Spirit*, edited by A. P. Castle.

The Lutheran Publishing House of Adelaide, Australia, for a prayer by Terry Falla from the compilation *Be Our Freedom*.

The British Broadcasting Corporation for a prayer from *New Every Morning*.

Curtis Brown Limited, New York, for the prayers of
Thomas Merton from *Thoughts in Solitude*.
McCrimmon Publishing Limited for prayers by Etta
Gullick and Michael Hollings, from *The Family Book
of Prayers*.
A. R. Mowbray for a prayer by Mother Teresa of
Calcutta from *The Wonder of Love*.
Augsburg Publishing House, Minneapolis, for a
prayer by J. Barrie Shepherd from *A Diary of
Private Prayer*.

Every effort has been made to ascribe the prayers
correctly and trace copyright holders; if there
should be any error or omission the publishers will
be happy to rectify this in any reprint.